The Commandment
We Forgot

TIM CHALLIES

CRUCIFORM PRESS | DECEMBER 2017

Cruciform
Quick

CruciformPress
@CHALLIES

AUTHOR

Tim Challies is a Christian, a husband to Aileen, and a father to three children aged 11 to 17. He is a co-founder of Cruciform Press and has written several books, including *Visual Theology*, *Do More Better*, and *Sexual Detox*. He worships and serves as a pastor at Grace Fellowship Church in Toronto, Ontario and writes daily at www.challies.com.

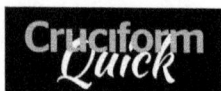

We all know the feeling: every week, every month, every year it just seems that life keeps moving faster and faster. So we've taken our trademark length—books of about 100 pages—and added a set of resources that will make for even a quicker read. Cruciform Quick: a new line of booklets in the range of 40 to 60 pages each.

THE COMMANDMENT WE FORGOT

Print / PDF ISBN: 978-1-941114-39-1
Mobipocket ISBN: 978-1-941114-40-7
ePub ISBN: 978-1-941114-41-4

Table of Contents

A Place of Special Honor

It is a commandment of God. It is a commandment with promise, connected to divine blessings. It is a commandment positioned in a place of special honor and significance. It is a commandment pertaining to the entire life of every human being. It is a commandment for the home, church, and workplace, providing a stable foundation for all of society. Yet it is a commandment that is sorely neglected. It may not be overstating the case to call it "the commandment we forgot." It is the fifth of God's ten great commandments to humanity: Honor your father and mother.

The purpose of this booklet is to explore how we can honor the fifth commandment and fulfill its obligations. In particular, we want to see how we can do this as adults. It's clear that the commandment applies to children. But does the commandment stop applying the day we move out or the day we get married? Does it expire when our parents die? Does it have any relevance for those whose parents prove themselves unworthy of respect through abandonment or abuse? Then there are the practical, urgent questions we must face: *What are my obligations toward my parents? Do I need to support them financially? Do I need to obey them even though I'm a full-grown adult?* These are some of the questions we need to answer if we wish to honor God by honoring his commandment.

I don't mind saying that I had high hopes for this booklet as I set out to research and write it. I'd like to think they have been realized. I wanted it to be biblical, depending on the Bible as the ultimate source of truth and the only authority that demands obedience and binds the conscience. I wanted it to be practical, answering real questions in real ways for real life. I wanted it to be multi-cultural, applying to readers from different contexts all around the world. I wanted it to be convicting, to impact and perhaps even transform the way we live. This is true whether we are young or old, whether we are parented or parenting, whether we are dependent upon our parents or they are dependent upon us, whether we live under their roof or whether they live under ours.

Our key verse will be Deuteronomy 5:16: "Honor your father and your mother, as the Lord your God commanded you, that your days may be long, and that it may go well with you in the land that the Lord your God is giving you." This verse will springboard us to other locations in the Old Testament: Exodus, which displays the terrible consequences of disobeying God's commandment, and Proverbs, which tells of God's promises of blessing to those who take his law seriously. And of course, we will go to the New Testament, to see how Jesus modeled and taught the way to honor parents, and to learn from Paul how ancient commands apply to contemporary believers.

I hope you will join me as we rediscover the commandment we forgot.

THREE REASONS TO KNOW AND OBEY THIS COMMANDMENT

Right away, we need to know why it is crucial that we know and obey the fifth commandment. Here are three reasons.

We are all children. It is the most basic biology. Every human being is the offspring of two other human beings.

Some of us have always known and respected both of our parents. Some have only ever known one biological parent. Some grew up with adoptive parents, and some were raised in foster care. Some of us have outlived our parents. Regardless, the fifth commandment applies to each of us for the simplest of reasons: we are all children. There is no human being outside of its purview because there is no parentless person.

We also know that God's commandments are to be taken both in their primary sense and as wider principles. The commandment's stipulations go beyond the simple relationship of children to parents and extend to all other God-given positions of authority. The right ordering of family government, church government, and civil government all depend on this commandment. In this way, too, it is universal. We are all children, we are all under authority, so we all need to hear and heed the fifth commandment.

This commandment comes with promise. Our second reason is that this commandment comes with promise. It is wise and good to obey the commandment so we can enjoy the promised blessings. Conversely, it is daft and dangerous to disobey the commandment and forfeit the promised blessings. When Paul writes to the children in Ephesus, he reminds them of God's promise for their obedience: "Children, obey your parents in the Lord, for this is right. 'Honor your father and mother' (this is the first commandment with a promise), 'that it may go well with you and that you may live long in the land'" (Ephesians 6:1-3). God promises a long life and a good life to those who obey this command. It pleases God when we obey, so naturally he dispenses his blessings to us (Colossians 3:20). We will explore the nature of these blessings soon.

God gives this commandment a place of special honor. Believers have long divided the ten commandments into two groups or two tables. The first group explains our duty toward

God and the second explains our duty toward our fellow men. This commandment falls squarely between the two, and in that way, it reminds us that our parents have a unique role in our lives. Our parents are God's divine representatives to us, so that when we honor and obey our parents we honor and obey God. We cannot say we obey and love God if we do not obey and love our parents. If we remove this commandment, we undermine all ten and fall into serious, dangerous disobedience.

We are all children, we ought to pursue God's blessings, and we need to give prominence to God's prominent command. For these reasons and many others, we can no longer ignore the forgotten commandment.

A WORD OF WARNING

Before we conclude this introduction, I would like to offer a word of warning. There is something deep within us that hears a commandment and immediately searches for the exception clause. *But you don't know my parents... But my parents disowned me... But my parents were abusive...* We will deal with exceptions and see how honor takes different forms in different situations. We will discuss what to do in cases of abuse or with especially contentious parents. But we must deal with the principle before we deal with the exceptions. I don't mean to excuse or downplay horrific experiences. But before we can do anything else we need to understand and admit this: there is no "if" attached to the fifth commandment. We must honor our parents. There are no exceptions.

WRAPPING UP

Let me close with a preview of what will follow as we progress through this booklet. In our first chapter we will explore God's promises of blessings and threats of judgment connected to the fifth commandment. Then we will consider honor and obedience as the basic ways we comply with the fifth commandment. We will then discuss the role of culture in understanding and obeying the commandment. We will look at very practical ways we can all honor God by honoring our parents. We will turn to hard cases like neglect, abuse, and abandonment—cases where honor is difficult or obedience would be sinful. And finally, we will discuss what it means to be a parent worthy of honor.

CHAPTER 1

Promises of Blessing, Threats of Judgment

As I prepared this booklet, I had extensive interactions with many people who had serious questions and concerns about the fifth commandment. I found that we are comfortable with its implications for children but perplexed with its implications for adults. How do we, as adults, show honor to our parents? What are our continuing obligations? What about parents who are difficult, absent, abusive, or even dead? What are the limitations on this commandment?

Before we come to satisfying answers for these questions, we must understand the seriousness with which God issues this commandment. In this chapter we will explore the benefits God promises to those who obey his commandment. Yet this means we also need to take a hard look at the ugly consequences he promises to those who disobey. When it comes to the relationship of children to their parents, the Bible holds out sweet promises of blessing but also terrible threats of judgment.

A COMMANDMENT WITH PROMISE

The Ten Commandments play a crucial role in our world. They teach human beings how to live in the way God means for us to live. The God who created us reveals his way to the fullest, most satisfying lives. These commandments tell rebellious and disordered people how to live in submission and order. The fifth commandment, then, speaks to people prone to rebel against authority—*all of us*, that is—and points us toward his good design: "Honor your father and your mother, as the LORD your God commanded you, that your days may be long, and that it may go well with you in the land that the LORD your God is giving you" (Deuteronomy 5:16).

Did you notice that God attaches blessings to this commandment? Writing centuries later, the Apostle Paul is careful to point these out: "Children, obey your parents in the Lord, for this is right. 'Honor your father and mother' (*this is the first commandment with a promise*), 'that it may go well with you and that you may live long in the land'" (Ephesians 6:1-3). Packed into these two sentences are three reasons children must honor their parents, as well as two great promises to those who do so.

Why should children honor their parents?

- *First, because nature demands it.* Paul says that "this is right." This is how God designed humanity, for children to honor their parents. All humans in all of time have this knowledge and this expectation.
- *Second, because God's law demands it.* Paul quotes the fifth commandment to show that God demands honor as an important part of his revealed will for humanity.
- *Third, because the gospel demands it.* Paul tells children to obey their parents "in the Lord." Those who have put their faith in the Lord are called to follow him in everything. The gospel assures children they can joyfully honor their parents, and the gospel gives them the motivation to actually do so.

What happens to those who heed nature, law, and gospel to honor their parents? God blesses them. "Honor your father and mother ... that it may go well with you and that you may live long in the land." God's blessing for those who obey the fifth commandment takes shape in two forms: a long life and a good life. These blessings are both a motive to obey and a natural consequence of such obedience.

A LONG LIFE, A GOOD LIFE

The Ten Commandments were given by God to a particular people in a unique context. In that day, long life in the Promised Land was symbolic of divine blessing. It was a sign that people were in God's favor, that they were experiencing the promised good life that comes with faithfulness to their covenant obligations. On the other hand, a shortened life or a life lived in exile were symbolic of divine disfavor, for these exemplified the curses that come with breaking their covenant obligations.

We need to understand, as did the Israelites, that these promises were not guarantees. God was not saying, "Honor your parents and I guarantee you will live to see at least eighty birthdays." Neither did he mean to communicate, "If you have a short life, it is proof you have dishonored your parents." Rather, he was saying that those who honor their parents generally experience a better life than those who do not. Why? Because those who honor their parents are doing things God's way, living in his good design.

What, then, is wrapped up in the promise of this good and long life? Dennis Rainey puts it this way: "Do you want to live with the favor of God upon you? Would you like to feel the blessing and the good hand of God upon your life? Then obey his commands."[1] He also points out a hidden benefit: honoring our parents helps complete our transition to adulthood. As we deliberately seek ways to honor our parents, we begin to reciprocate the love they have given us since birth. We complete the relationship by reaching out in love to them just as they have always reached out to us. The love, the care, the honor, is now mutual, just the way God intends it. We have grown up.

A SHORT LIFE, A MISERABLE LIFE

While the fifth commandment lays out the terms of blessing for obedience, it implies the consequences for disobedience. These consequences are spelled out in greater detail elsewhere in the Bible, first in the civil law and then in the Old Testament's wisdom literature.

As God revealed the law that would govern the nation of Israel, he included a penalty for those who would flagrantly and unrepentantly violate the fifth commandment. It may shock us to realize this penalty was the same for murder and other horrendous crimes.

- Whoever strikes his father or his mother shall be put to death. Whoever curses his father or his mother shall be put to death. (Exodus 21:15, 17)
- For anyone who curses his father or his mother shall surely be put to death; he has cursed his father or his mother; his blood is upon him. (Leviticus 20:9)
- If a man has a stubborn and rebellious son who will not obey the voice of his father or the voice of his mother, and, though they discipline him, will not listen to them, then his father and his mother shall take hold of him and bring him out to the elders of his city at the gate of the place where he lives, and they shall say to the elders of his city, "This our son is stubborn and rebellious; he will not obey our

voice; he is a glutton and a drunkard." Then all the
men of the city shall stone him to death with stones.
So you shall purge the evil from your midst, and all
Israel shall hear, and fear. (Deuteronomy 21:18-21)

To think that rebellion from today's children and teen-
agers is normal! To think that we now take this kind of defiance so lightly! God's law shows just how seriously he takes
the fifth commandment. How is it, then, that we treat it so
flippantly?

The book of Proverbs further displays the horrible consequences of dishonoring parents:

- He who does violence to his father and chases away
  his mother is a son who brings shame and reproach.
  (Proverbs 19:26)
- If one curses his father or his mother, his lamp will
  be put out in utter darkness. (Proverbs 20:20)
- The eye that mocks a father and scorns to obey a
  mother will be picked out by the ravens of the valley
  and eaten by the vultures. (Proverbs 30:17)

Though portrayed in poetic language, the picture is clear:
there are the sweetest blessings stored up for those who
obey the fifth commandment, and there are the most terrible
judgments stored up for those who do not. God expects and
demands that children will honor their parents.

THE DUTY OF HONOR

You and I do not live in ancient Israel. We are no longer
under the civil laws of God's nation. Yet God's blessings still
extend to us. After all, Paul freely assured children that God

would bless them as they honored their parents. They would acknowledge, as we do, that the promise of land is no longer valid. But the general rule remains: if we live in God's ways we receive God's favor, and if we defy God's ways we forfeit God's favor. Honor God by honoring your parents and expect it will go well with you. Dishonor God by dishonoring your parents and expect it will not. It's the way God has structured his world.

CHAPTER 2

Momentary Obedience, Forever Honor

We have looked at the sweet blessings God promises to those who heed the fifth commandment, and we have looked at the terrible judgments he promises to those who do not. We have seen that children have a lifelong duty of honor toward their parents. But while we have learned *why* we ought to honor our parents, we have not yet considered *how*. Our question for this chapter is this: How do we show honor to our parents, especially when we are adults?

HONOR AND OBEY

In both descriptions of the Ten Commandments—those found in Exodus and Deuteronomy—God commands children, "Honor your father and your mother." There is not a word about obedience. Yet when we read the applications of the commandment scattered throughout the Bible, we see obedience as a key component of the honor children owe their parents. This raises questions: Is obedience to parents permanent, or is it temporary? Does honor always require obedience? If I want to honor my parents do I need to continue obeying them into adulthood? To answer these questions we need to examine honor and obedience, looking for what makes them similar and what distinguishes them.

OBEY

What the fifth commandment does not require is as important as what it does require. The fifth commandment is not, "*Obey* your father and your mother." Rather it is, "*Honor* your father and your mother." Still, the Bible clearly places a great deal of emphasis on children obeying parents.

We encounter the language of obedience in many of the interpretations and applications of the fifth commandment. Yet as we dig deeper, we find something interesting: the language of obedience tends to come only in passages speaking to young children who are still dependent upon their parents. When we come to passages speaking to adult children, we find a subtle switch to language of respect and provision. Thus, obedience is a particular form of honor—a form of honor for young children.

All children are to honor their parents at all times. But when children are young, honor most often takes the form of obedience. This is why Paul references the fifth commandment and tells young children to "obey your parents" (Ephesians 6:1-3, Colossians 3:20). To obey is to submit to the will of a person who rightfully holds a position of authority, to comply with their demands or their requests. As my wife and I teach our children, obedience means "do it now, do it right, and do it with a happy heart." Obedience is a child's display of honor.

Parents are right to expect and demand obedience of their children, and children are right to show honor to their parents through that obedience. Obedience to parents trains children to be submissive to every other authority, including God himself. It is under the training and discipline of parents that children are prepared to live orderly lives in this world. John MacArthur says it well: "Children who respect and obey their parents will build a society that is ordered, harmonious, and productive. A generation of undisciplined, disobedient children will produce a society that is chaotic and destructive."[2]

Children are meant to obey their parents as long as they are under the authority of their parents. Parents teach their children to obey so that they will learn to honor—and spend the rest of their lives honoring—parents, teachers, bosses, governments, and, ultimately, God.

HONOR

But what is honor? Biblically, the word honor refers to weight or significance. Honoring our parents means attaching great worth to them and great value to our relationship with them. John Currid explains, "The point is that a child must not take his or her parents lightly, or think lightly of them. They must be regarded with great seriousness and value."[3] We can learn about honor by reading passages that describe dishonorable behavior. These are the passages from the civil law and wisdom literature we looked at in our last chapter: Leviticus 20:9, Proverbs 30:17, and so on.

What do we find? Children who dishonor their parents are rebellious and stubbornly resistant to the discipline that would lead them out of that rebellion. They may be verbally abusive, mocking and cursing their parents. They may even be physically violent toward them. If we turn to the New Testament, we find that their dishonor may take the form of refusing to care for their parents or failing to provide for their physical and monetary needs (Mark 7:8-13, 1 Timothy 5:8).

Thus, to honor our parents we are to respect and revere them, speak well of them, and treat them with kindness, gentleness, and dignity. We are to ensure they are cared for and provide for them when necessary. Dennis Rainey says, "Honor is an attitude accompanied by actions that say to your parents, 'You are worthy. You have value. You are the person God sovereignly placed in my life.'"[4] All of that and much more is bound up in this little word.

OBEY TODAY, HONOR FOREVER

We need to consider why the basic requirement of the fifth commandment is not obedience but honor. I am convinced there are at least two reasons: eventually we are no longer obligated to obey our parents and, even before then, there are times we cannot or must not obey them. To say it another way, there are times we can disobey our parents while still honoring them.

The end of obedience. There comes a time when obeying parents is no longer appropriate. The task of parents is to raise their children to become independent, to function outside of parental authority. In most cases, the parent-child relationship will be permanently altered at the moment of marriage when "a man shall leave his father and his mother and hold fast to his wife" (Genesis 2:24). As a child becomes independent of his parents, he leaves their oversight and authority. He no longer owes obedience in the same way or to the same degree.

The sin of obedience. There may also be occasions when obedience is sinful, such as when parents command their children to sin, or when they command their children to disobey government. When this happens a child must disobey their parent's authority in order to obey God's authority. Another occasion for acceptable disobedience is when parents demand obedience of their adult children, or when their demands for obedience become abusive. In such cases the child is under no God-given obligation to obey.

God's basic command to humanity is not, "Obey your

father and mother," since obedience ends and can sometimes be sinful. Instead, God's command is, "Honor your father and mother," because honor never ends and is never wrong.

PERFECT HONOR, PERFECT OBEDIENCE

We are not without a biblical model of honor and obedience. We see them both perfectly displayed in Jesus. Though he was God, he was born to earthly parents and he willingly, joyfully, perfectly honored and obeyed them both. We see his child-hood obedience in Luke 2:51: "And he went down with them and came to Nazareth and was submissive to them." We see his honor when, in the moments before his death, he ensured provision for his mother: "When Jesus saw his mother and the disciple whom he loved standing nearby, he said to his mother, 'Woman, behold, your son!' Then he said to the disciple, 'Behold, your mother!' And from that hour the disciple took her to his own home" (John 19:26-27).

And just as Jesus honored and obeyed his earthly mother and father, he honored and obeyed his heavenly Father. He always spoke well of his Father, directed glory to his Father, and revered his Father. And of course, Jesus obeyed him in everything: "For I have come down from heaven, not to do my own will but the will of him who sent me" (John 6:38).

Jesus honored and obeyed God by honoring and obeying his earthly parents. If we want to honor and obey our parents we must learn about Jesus. If we want our children to honor and obey us, we must teach them about Jesus. As always, he is the example of how to perfectly obey God's perfect law.

CHAPTER 3

One Man's Honor Is Another Man's Shame

A video titled "Asian Parents React To 'I Love You'"[5] went viral a few years ago. It featured a number of Asian young adults telling their parents, "I love you," and recording their parents' response. Why did this video go viral? Because saying and hearing "I love you" is uncommon in many Asian cultures. It's not that Asian parents and children don't love one another, of course, but that love and honor are displayed in other ways. These children were surprising their parents by something that would seem unremarkable in many other parts of the world.

In this examination of the fifth commandment—"Honor your father and your mother"—we have come to the place where we need to speak about culture. We have already seen that children owe their parents a life-long debt of honor, but we have only hinted at how honor is displayed in different ways across different contexts. Our goal is to find ways that each of us can express the honor we owe our parents, but we can only do that when we have first accounted for cultural differences.

I have the joy of living in what may be the world's most multicultural city. Even my own small church has representatives from at least 30 different cultures, and much of the research for this chapter has come from interviews with them. Interviews included discussions with people representing Belarus, Canada, El Salvador, Ghana, India, Iraq, Jamaica, Philippines, and South Korea. After examining the differences and similarities among these contexts, I distilled them into two broad groupings, two kinds of culture, each of which has very different ways of honoring parents.

A CULTURE OF AUTONOMY

The first kind of culture values autonomy and independence as high virtues. Parents expect to eventually regain their independence as their children leave the home, and they look forward to a retirement of ease and entertainment. All the while their children look forward to gaining permanent independence from their parents. This culture tends to idealize the fun and freedom of youth, while dreading the responsibilities of adulthood. Age is not associated with wisdom and respect, but with fear or even mockery at the loss of physical and mental faculties. Aging adults dread the impending loss of independence.

This culture has few fixed expectations for how adult children are to honor their aging parents. Parents may expect little more than regular phone calls and visits on major holidays. As parents get older, children may become involved in their care, but they typically do not move parents into their home and become primary caregivers. Instead, as parents age, they are expected to move to retirement or nursing facilities, where they will live out their final days.

When it comes to finances, parents are to support their children until they become independent, but there is little expectation that children will return the favor later in life. Instead, parents are to diligently save for their own retirement and fund it themselves. When parents do need to be cared for, that responsibility is distributed among willing children and does not fall to a particular child based on sex or birth order.

These low expectations are shared by parents and children

alike. One interviewee said, "My parents told me that when they are old, we should just move them to a nursing home. They would hate to disrupt our lives in any way." Grown children do not wish to go through the trouble of caring for their parents. Elderly parents do not wish to inconvenience their children by needing care. If there is shame in this culture, it is attached to parents who have not diligently saved to provide for their own care.

A CULTURE OF AUTHORITY

Another kind of culture values honor and respect as high virtues, while dreading and avoiding whatever brings shame. These cultures respect the elderly, associating age with wisdom and authority and associating youth with folly. They often have terms or titles for those who are older and customs to show respect and deference to elders. These cultures place lower value on independence and autonomy and much greater value on duty toward family.

Honor is displayed in obedience and sacrifice, while shame comes from disobedience and selfishness. Thus even adult children are expected to honor their parents by spending time with them and involving them in their daily lives. Honor means not only seeking their wisdom in major life decisions, but also heeding their counsel. And just as parents have sacrificed for their children, children are later to reciprocate with sacrifices that will benefit their parents. The actions or behavior of children of any age will enhance or diminish the family's reputation.

There is typically a strong hierarchy within the family where the eldest son (or eldest child in some cultures) bears the weightiest responsibility for care and provision. It is expected that as his parents age, he will welcome them into his home, for this brings honor to both the child and his parents. To put his parents in a retirement or nursing facility would bring great shame to the whole family—shame to the child for not fulfilling his duty and shame to the parents for not raising their child well.

TWO WAYS OF HONOR

These are very broad descriptions, of course, but I suspect you can recognize these two kinds of culture. The autonomy culture exists mostly in Westernized nations, while the authority culture exists within honor-or-shame societies, which encompass most of the earth's population. The differences between them are pronounced to say the least.

Consider this: a North American adult can say, "My parents live in a retirement home," and people will think the family has done something good and noble. The parents are glad they saved diligently and can afford to be in a nice retirement community, and the children are glad their parents are cared for by professionals and surrounded by people in the same life stage. But if an Indian adult says, "My parents live in a retirement home," their Indian peers will be horrified and think the family has done something woefully shameful. After all, the child is refusing to fulfill his obligations, which demonstrates that his parents did not raise him well. Now those parents are cared for by cold professionals rather than loving children, and they are surrounded by strangers rather than family members. One culture's honor is another culture's shame. This forces us to grapple with a couple of considerations.

First, our cultural presuppositions may be wrong. But as long as we fail to recognize that much of our decision-making is guided by cultural norms rather than biblical guidelines, we cannot discern which of our cultural practices are wrong.

One kind of culture may demand too little, while the other may demand too much. One culture may legitimize dishonor while another may idolize honor. As Christians we need to think carefully and biblically, rather than simply accepting what the culture dictates. It is possible that Western children will have to make efforts to convince their parents they ought to be honored, while people from other cultures may need to refuse to conform to some of the expectations placed upon them.

Second, we need to show honor in ways that are appropriate to our culture and meaningful to our parents, while still remaining faithful to Scripture. Thus the way I show honor to my parents may look very different from my Ghanaian or Cuban friend sitting next to me at Grace Fellowship Church. I don't necessarily need to honor my parents in a Ghanian way, and my friends don't necessarily need to honor their parents in a Canadian way. We can and should learn from one another, but without judgment for what may seem like either dishonor or over-honor.

CHAPTER 4

Practical Ways to Honor Your Parents

God's commandments are perfectly clear in what they say and in what they broadly require. Yet obeying these commandments in practical ways and in the nitty-gritty of life can pose a challenge. It can take thought, prayer, creativity. This is exactly the case with the fifth commandment—"Honor your father and your mother"—and especially so for adult children. Young children honor their parents through their obedience, but what about adults? How do we honor our parents in ways that are fitting?

I've waited a few chapters to get to this point in this booklet, and my slow pace has been deliberate. We tend to skip over foundational matters to get straight to the practical stuff. Just give me the list of things to do, and I'll do them! But true transformation and the right application will only come when we first take time to understand God's commandment—what it means, why he gives it, why it matters so much. We are now ready to consider practical ways we can honor our parents.

HONOR TO WHOM HONOR IS DUE

In an earlier chapter, I pointed out that honoring parents is a form of honoring all authority, including God himself. As Tim Keller says, "It's respect for parents that is the basis for every other kind of respect and every other kind of authority."[6] I have pointed out as well that there is no ending point to this commandment—we are to honor our parents in childhood and adulthood, for we owe them a debt of honor that never ends.

What is the honor God means for us to give our parents? I am going to offer six broad suggestions, though certainly we could come up with many more. I will warn in advance: in every case there will be temptations to say, "Yes, but you don't know my parents. You don't know who they are or what they did to me." I understand that in some cases, showing honor may be difficult or very nearly impossible. In the next chapter we will discuss some hard cases. But for now, let's simply consider some practical ways we can display honor to our parents.

FORGIVE THEM

Perhaps the most important way we can honor our parents is to forgive them. There are no perfect parents. All parents have fallen far short of their children's expectations and, in all likelihood, their own expectations. Our parents have sinned against us. They have made unwise decisions, they have had unrealistic expectations, they have said and done things that have left us deeply wounded. For that reason, many children enter adulthood controlled by anger and bitterness. They find themselves unable to move past their parents' mistakes and sins.

We can best honor our parents by forgiving our parents. And this is actually possible, for we serve and imitate a forgiving Savior. On the cross, Jesus died for the sins of those who had wounded him. In the very moment the nails were driven into his flesh, he cried out, "Father, forgive them, for they know not what they do" (Luke 23:34). Standing at the foot of the cross and considering such a Savior, who are we to withhold forgiveness from our parents? We honor our parents by extending grace and forgiveness to them.

SPEAK WELL OF THEM

Another way we can honor our parents is to speak well of them and refuse to speak evil of them. We live at a time when it is considered noble to air our grievances, when it is considered therapeutic to air our dirty laundry. We think little of telling the world exactly what we think of our governors, our bosses, our parents. Yet the Bible warns us that we owe honor and respect to all of the authorities God has placed over us (Romans 13:7). It warns us that our words have the power to extend honor or dishonor. We cannot miss that in the Old Testament the penalty for cursing parents is the same as the penalty for assaulting them, for the root sin is the same (Exodus 21:15-17, Leviticus 20:9). To curse parents or to strike parents is to violate the fifth commandment.

We need to speak well of our parents. We need to speak well of them while they are alive and speak well of them after they have died. We need to speak well of them to our siblings, to our spouses, to our children. We need to speak well of them to our churches and communities, modeling a counter-cultural kind of honor and respect that has long since gone missing. Christian, speak well of your parents and refuse to speak evil of them.

ESTEEM THEM PUBLICLY AND PRIVATELY

A third way to show honor to parents is to hold them in high esteem both privately and publicly. In a powerful sermon on the fifth commandment, Tim Keller says that children need to "respect their [parents'] need to see themselves in you." Parents long to see how they have impacted their children, how their children are a reflection of their strengths, their values. "You don't realize how important it is to give them credit where you can. You don't realize how critical it is just to say, 'You know, everything I really ever learned about saving money I learned from you.' To say, 'You know, Dad, that was one thing you always taught me that I really, really appreciated.'"[7] These are simple measures, but ones that bring great joy and honor to our parents.

We can give such esteem privately in one-on-one conversation, or we can do this publicly, perhaps through speeches or sermons or conversations around holiday dinners. Dennis Rainey calls children to write a formal tribute to their parents, to present it to them, and to read it aloud in their presence.[8] We can honor our parents by esteeming our parents.

SEEK THEIR WISDOM

We honor our parents when we seek their wisdom through life's twists and turns. The Bible constantly associates youth with folly and age with wisdom and tells us that those who have lived longer lives have generally accumulated greater wisdom (Proverbs 20:29, Job 12:12). We do well, then, to lean on our parents for understanding, to seek their input when faced with major decisions. In some cultures this is expected, and in some it is eschewed. But this is an example where biblical wisdom ought to take precedence over cultural norms. It honors our parents when we seek their help, even if in the end we should not or cannot heed it.

SUPPORT THEM

We can also honor our parents by supporting them. I am not yet speaking of financial support, but other forms of love and care. I think of David, weighed down by cares and the attacks of his enemies, crying out to God, "Do not cast me off in the time of old age; forsake me not when my strength is spent" (Psalm 71:9). David feared the loneliness that often accompanies old age. So, too, do our elderly parents.

When we are young we need our parents' help, and we long for independence. Our parents raise us to be strong and free. But there is a trade-off here, a passing of the baton, for as our parents age they become feeble and begin to lose their independence (Ecclesiastes 12:1-8). We honor our parents by giving them the assurance that we will not forsake them in their old age. Just as they cared for us, we will care for them. This is our responsibility, and it ought to be our joy.

At a time when millions of elderly adults are living alone, consigned to nursing homes and hospitals, cared for by professionals rather than family members, Christians have the opportunity to display special honor. Bryan Chapell and Kent Hughes say that even if parents have no financial needs, "there is still a Christian obligation for hands-on, loving care. Nurses may be employed, but there must be more—the care cannot be done by proxy. Emotional neglect and abandonment is not an option, for such conduct 'is worse than an unbeliever.'"[9]

PROVIDE FOR THEM

Finally, we can honor our parents by providing for them financially. In Paul's first letter to Timothy, he gives instructions on how to honor widows within the church. He gives two important principles: children are to make some return to their parents, and Christians who will not provide for family members are behaving worse than unbelievers (1 Timothy 5:4, 8). Commentators are nearly unanimous in extending these principles to children and their elderly parents. What is unremarkable in some cultures is controversial in others, including my own. Stott points out that "African and Asian cultures, which have developed the extended in place of the nuclear family, are a standing rebuke to the West in this matter."[10]

When children are young, God expects parents to provide for them (2 Corinthians 12:14), but in time children are to be willing to reciprocate. Families are to hold together in this way, caring for one another when young *and* old. When parents are strong and children are weak, the parents are to provide. When children are strong and parents are weak, the children are to provide. Perhaps no form of honor cuts more deeply against the Western grain than this one. But it's clear: God calls Christians to take special responsibility for providing for their family members. This command applies equally to the parents of young children and the children of elderly parents. Because this principle is so foreign to Western culture, I dedicate the next chapter to it.

CHAPTER 5

The Tricky Matter of Money

Crash Course Philosophy has more than 5 million subscribers, making it one of the most popular YouTube channels. One of their popular videos is "Family Obligations," in which they explain the view of American philosopher Jane English that grown children have no obligation to their parents and should feel no duty to care for them or even to remain in relationship. Essentially, because children do not choose to be born, they bear no obligation toward the people who chose to conceive them. Good parents give love unconditionally with no expectation of reciprocation. The more appropriate model to govern relationships of parents to their grown children is friendship, says English. Friendships are freely chosen and allow children to care for their parents out of choice rather than obligation.[11]

Such a view sounds harsh, but while few people would explain it in such blunt terms, it is common in the Western world. We assume that parents should raise their children to be independent and that children should then be free of further obligation, especially when it comes to finances. As Christians, we need to look beyond philosophy and look instead to the Bible for our guidance.

AN OBLIGATION OF HONOR

According to the Ten Commandments, children are obligated to honor their parents. "Honor your father and your mother, as the LORD your God commanded you, that your days may be long, and that it may go well with you in the land that the LORD your God is giving you" (Deuteronomy 5:16). This honor is demanded of young children, of course, but equally of grown children. It is an obligation that never ends. But does honor include financial provision? The Bible makes it clear that it does. We can see this by a brief examination of two relevant passages.

MAKE SOME RETURN

In 1 Timothy 5, Paul writes to Timothy to explain how the church is to care for older widows who are no longer able to provide for themselves. He explains that the church has an obligation to care for them, but that this obligation is secondary to that of her family. "Honor widows who are truly widows. But if a widow has children or grandchildren, let them first learn to show godliness to their own household and to make some return to their parents, for this is pleasing in the sight of God" (1 Timothy 5:3-4). The church is to care for a widow only when her family is unwilling or unable to do so.

Why must the family take primary responsibility? Paul offers a list of five reasons. First, it is a display of godliness for a Christian to care for his own family members. Generosity with time, attention, and money shows that the person is living for the good of others rather than the good of self. Second, it is right for children to "make some return" to their parents for the care and provision they once received. As commentator William Barcley says, "The raising of children requires tremendous sacrifice and it is only right that children make sacrifices for parents in return."[12] Third, it pleases God. The God who so carefully and intimately cares for our needs is pleased when we give loving attention to the needs of others.

In verse 8, Paul adds a sobering fourth reason: "But if anyone does not provide for his relatives, and especially for members of his household, he has denied the faith and is worse than an unbeliever." Here, Paul makes an appeal to natural law. Even unbelievers know that they are to care for their parents, for God has written this on their hearts (Romans 2:15). Christians know this twice—by natural law and by God's revealed law in the Bible. The Christian who refuses to heed both forms of law has denied the practical implications of the faith and, in that way, made himself worse than an unbeliever.

Finally, he provides a fifth reason: to relieve the burden on the church. "If any believing woman has relatives who are widows, let her care for them. Let the church not be burdened, so that it may care for those who are truly widows" (1 Timothy 5:16). If the church can release the burden of care to the family, it frees resources that can now be used to care for those who have no family.

MAKING VOID THE WORD OF GOD

The second relevant passage is in Mark 7, where Jesus challenges the religious authorities for rigidly adhering to a man-made law that contradicts the law of God. Jesus said,

> You have a fine way of rejecting the commandment of God in order to establish your tradition! For Moses said, "Honor your father and your mother"; and, "Whoever reviles father or mother must surely die." But you say, "If a man tells his father or his mother, 'Whatever you would have gained from me is Corban'" (that is, given to God)—then you no longer permit him to do anything for his father or mother, thus making void the word of God by your tradition that you have handed down. And many such things you do. (Mark 7:9-13)

These religious leaders were declaring their possessions "Corban," vowing to dedicate them to God so that after their death all they owned would become the property of the temple. Yet in doing so they were making two grave errors. First, they were neglecting a primary responsibility in favor of a secondary one. Giving their wealth to the temple may have been a good thing to do, but it was less important than their duty to provide for their parents. Second, they were deliberately withholding support from their parents out of anger or spite. T.W. Manson explains "Corban" in this way: "A man goes through the formality of vowing something to God, not that he may give it to God, but in order to prevent some other person from having it."[13] Mark Strauss concludes, "Jesus condemns this use of *qorbān*, not just because honor for parents supersedes vow-taking, but because the selfish motives behind such traditions are contrary to the heart of God and the true spirit of the law."[14]

HONOR AND PROVIDE

Let's conclude with four points of application.

First, children have an obligation to give life-long honor to their parents, and this honor includes financial provision when necessary. This is backed up by the weight of biblical scholarship. Douglas Milne says, "When the children are dependent on the parents, it is right that the parents should provide for the children, but the roles are reversed in later years when the parents become dependent on their children." MacArthur says much the same: "[Children] owe a debt to those who brought them into the world, clothed them, fed them, housed them, supported them, and loved and nurtured them."[15] Honor is more than provision, but not less than provision.

Second, there may be extenuating circumstances that will need to be navigated with wisdom and discernment, and perhaps under the guidance of local church leaders. Some forms of provision may actually enable addiction or abhorrent behavior. Some parents may demand financial help when they are still capable of providing for themselves. Some parents may have so damaged their children that financial support is especially difficult. Prayerful, biblically informed elders can help bring clarity to such complexity.

Third, a Christian who refuses to care for his parents or close family members has sinned to the degree that he should not be surprised when his church puts him under discipline. The person who will not take on this responsibility has "denied the faith" and made himself "worse than an unbeliever." These are serious charges that are unworthy of one who claims to follow the Savior who was sure to provide for his own mother (John 19:27).

CHAPTER 6

When Honor Is Hard

The motivation behind this booklet was the knowledge that few of us seriously consider the fifth commandment and how we can actively fulfill it, even after we have left our parents' authority. We have been focusing on Deuteronomy 5:16: "Honor your father and your mother, as the LORD your God commanded you, that your days may be long, and that it may go well with you in the land that the LORD your God is giving you." We have already seen that this commandment is not only for children. At every age, we owe our parents a debt of honor and this can be expressed in a number of ways: forgiving our parents, speaking well of them, esteeming them publicly and privately, seeking their wisdom, supporting them, and providing for them.

Well and good. That's straightforward enough when we have a good relationship with our parents, when they raised us well, when they loved and respected us. But what about people who were adopted and never knew their birth parents? What about people who had difficult or absent or abusive parents? What about people whose parents behaved in utterly dishonorable ways? Does this debt of honor extend even to them? In all the feedback I've received on this topic, more has focused on these concerns than any other. "Do you really expect me to honor my parents? Let me tell you about them..."

I have approached this chapter with caution, with prayer, with Bible in hand. All the while I have been thinking about people I know and love, many of them in my own church, who have had to navigate excruciating situations. And as far as I can see, all children are to extend honor to their parents.

There are no exception clauses. I acknowledge that in some cases honor will be extremely difficult. I acknowledge that in some cases damage runs very deep. I acknowledge some past traumas cannot and must not be overlooked. And yet I still believe there is a debt of honor we all owe our parents.

A DIFFERENT CONTEXT FOR HONOR

I want to begin by briefly changing our context. Parents are not the only people God tells us we must honor. They are not the only source of authority we may struggle to honor. In Romans 13, Paul writes about civil authorities and says this: "Pay to all what is owed to them: taxes to whom taxes are owed, revenue to whom revenue is owed, respect to whom respect is owed, honor to whom honor is owed" (7). It is important to acknowledge that Paul wrote these words while under the reign of tyrannical Roman rulers. Yet even in this context he exhorted the believers of his day to honor and respect the government.

Douglas Moo points out that the history of the interpretation of this passage "is the history of attempts to avoid what seems to be its plain meaning" and warns that "we must not obscure [its meaning] in a flood of qualifications." The passages teaches that all authority is ultimately an extension of God's divine authority delegated to human beings, for "there is no authority except from God" (Romans 13:1a). It also teaches that all authority is a display of God's sovereignty, for "those [authorities] that exist have been instituted by God" (Romans 13:1b). There is a kind of honor we owe whether or not the other party has earned it. It is theirs by virtue of a God-given position. Moo concludes, "Government is more than a nuisance to be put up with; it is an institution established by

God to accomplish some of his purposes on earth."[16] There-fore, when we honor our rulers we honor God, and when we dishonor our rulers we dishonor God.

FROM GOVERNMENT TO FAMILY

Much of what is true of civil authorities must be true of parents as well. Just as God's sovereignty is displayed in elevating rulers to lead a nation, God's sovereignty is displayed in choosing parents to give birth to a child. Just as God delegates authority and responsibility to government, God delegates authority and responsibility to parents. Just as God expects we will honor government as an extension of his authority and sovereignty, he expects we will honor parents as an extension of his authority and sovereignty. Just as honoring rulers is honoring God, so honoring parents is honoring God. We must give to our rulers and to our parents all that is owed them, including honor. There is no exception for bad governments or bad parents.

HONORING THE DISHONORABLE

So how do we honor parents who have behaved dishonorably and abhorrently? This will sometimes be very difficult. This will often require us to exercise great wisdom and walk very fine lines. Without knowing individual cases, speaking broadly can be both difficult and dangerous. Thankfully, God puts us under the care of pastors and shepherds to help us navigate difficulties like these, and we do well to seek their care and counsel. I will offer some general suggestions, but I would also ask you to think and pray and approach others to gain their wisdom. In the specific case of abuse, Dennis Rainey offers wise guidance in his book on the fifth commandment. In the meantime, here are some distinctions to consider.

Distinguish between honor and obedience. In an earlier chapter we learned that honor does not always include obedience. When parents demand what God forbids, we must defer to the higher authorities of God or government. When parents overstep their bounds and demand obedience of adult children, we may also refuse to obey them. But even while we refuse to obey, we can still give honor. Rather than exploding in anger or making a great show of defiance, we can respond with dignity, calmness, and respect, yet still with iron resolve. This may not make our parents' response any better, but at least we will have been blameless in God's sight.

Distinguish between the person and the position. Even if honoring our parents through a relationship would be impossible or unwise, we can still honor fatherhood and motherhood as positions. We can learn how the Bible describes God's design for parents and determine that we will only speak well of them. The military demands soldiers respect the rank if not the man, and to some degree we can do the same with parents—honoring the position when we can't find anything honorable in the person. The adopted child may have never known his birth parents, but he can still avoid speaking evil of them, and he can still speak well of motherhood and fatherhood.

Distinguish between honor and relationship. In some cases past actions have been so utterly deplorable that a child must break from his or her parents. For example, God does not demand that children who were sexually abused by their unrepentant fathers remain in close relationship with them into adulthood. Perhaps the best they can do to honor God in this situation is to refuse to dishonor their parents. In such cases, honoring God may mean honestly facing the trauma, leaving vengeance in his hands, and acknowledging before God that he made no mistakes in choosing the parents. It may mean extending forgiveness to parents (if they have sought it) or at least a willingness to forgive them (if they have not). It means letting go of bitterness, trusting God through the pain, and dwelling deeply on the display of his compassion on the cross. At the very least it is absolving God of all blame for what happened and trusting that these things did not happen apart from his sovereignty.

Distinguish between honor and agreement. Some children are concerned that honoring parents means agreement with odious positions they hold. A child whose parents are racist may believe that honoring her parents indicates tolerance with those racist beliefs. Yet honor can be extended in such a way that it is genuine, but still resolute. After all, we are called to honor our pro-choice governments even while holding firmly to pro-life positions and challenging the government to change. Honoring our parents does not necessarily mean approval of everything they have done or everything they believe.

Distinguish between honor and enabling. Honoring your parents does not mean enabling their sin or sinful patterns. It does not mean covering up what they did or continue to do or hiding it from civil authorities. Those who were abused will do no dishonor to their parents if they make that abuse known and seek to have their parents prosecuted to the furthest extent of the law.

These are five distinctions that may prove helpful as we consider the hard cases. Yet we must be aware that they could also prove dangerous. We must take care that we don't slip into a definition of honor so narrow as to be meaningless. As individuals convinced of the need to honor our parents, we need to meditate on Deuteronomy 5:16, Romans 13:1-7, and other key passages, then respond to God's conviction. He will help us, he will guide us to all truth, to all obedience (John 16:13).

HONOR TO WHOM HONOR IS OWED

The more I read and study Scripture, the more I conclude that God asks impossible things of his people. At least, he asks things that would be impossible without his presence, his wisdom, and his power. In the hard cases, giving honor to parents may seem impossible. But still the call goes out: "Give ... honor to whom honor is owed." For many people this is the deepest kind of challenge. For all of us, it is a challenge for which we would desperately need the grace of God.

CHAPTER 7

A Parent Who Is Worthy of Honor

We are drawing near the end of our exploration of the fifth commandment and, in particular, how adult children are to obey it. "Honor your father and your mother, as the LORD your God commanded you, that your days may be long, and that it may go well with you in the land that the LORD your God is giving you." While heeding this command is relatively straightforward for young children under the authority of their parents, it is much more difficult to know what it entails for adult children. Through this booklet, we have learned how such honor can be given. We have seen that all children owe their parents a debt of honor that continues past childhood. All children of all ages are to honor their parents. We have explored this from many angles and now, as we conclude, I want to explore it from just one more.

Children do not bear the full responsibility of the fifth commandment. If children are to extend honor to their parents, parents are to make it easy for them by living honorable lives. We need to repeat what we have said before: children are not to wait until their parents prove honorable before extending honor, for the parents' honor derives from their position, not their behavior. Yet there is still an onus on the parent to live a worthy and respectable life. And this is what I wish to consider in this chapter: How can we who are parents live lives that are worthy of honor? How can we make it easy for our children to honor us now and in the future?

THE GLORY OF CHILDREN

Proverbs 17:6 tells us, "Grandchildren are the crown of the aged, and the glory of children is their fathers." It is the second half of this proverb that is of particular interest to me. What does it mean that "the glory of children is their fathers"? Even while we must acknowledge a unique Old Testament context, we can still agree with Eric Lane who says, "For the children themselves their greatest blessing was to have parents in whom they could take pride—respected in the community, prosperous in business and thorough in bringing them up."[17] It is a blessing for children to have honorable parents, and it is right for them to take pride in their fathers and, of course, in their mothers as well.

In John Kitchen's commentary on the proverb, he emphasizes the importance of parents living with honor:

> Children find great honor in having an honorable father. True, the commandment requires children to honor their father and mother (Exodus 20:12), but it is also incumbent upon the father to give his children reason to do so. What greater earthly incentive could there be to live honorably as a man, than to have your children be proud of you and long to model your character? [18]

Parents are the pride of children when they live honorably.

LIVING HONORABLY

How do parents live honorably? There are a hundred possibilities, a hundred ways to answer. We could create a list of characteristics that ought to mark the Christian parent: love, kindness, patience, gentleness. We could generate a list of duties that parents ought to fulfill: spending quality time with our children, praying for them, reading God's Word to them. We could come up with a list of characteristics and behaviors to avoid: do not exasperate our children, do not treat them unfairly, do not fail to raise them in the discipline and instruction of the Lord. The possibilities are endless. I intend to keep it simple and propose three areas of emphasis.

First, make your own godliness your foremost concern. As parents, there is the tendency to expect more from our children than we expect from ourselves. We have great expectations for them but only modest expectations for ourselves. A life of honor before others begins with a life of honor before God. As we pursue God, we will long to be who he wants us to be, to put on all the noble characteristics associated with godliness and to put off all the ugly characteristics associated with ungodliness. We will want to behave how God means for us to behave, to put aside any actions that are unfitting for a Christian while emphasizing all those actions that are worthy of a Christian. In these ways we will model mature character and behavior, extending and displaying love to our children, even when they exasperate us or push us to the brink of despair. We will live with a clear conscience before God, man, and our own children.

Second, identify and imitate worthy models. Especially within the local church, look for people who have modeled successful parenting. God has put us in local church communities so we can receive help through all of life's challenges and difficulties. God surrounds us with other believers so we can observe honorable models to imitate. Be deliberate in identifying people whose children love and honor them, whose children delight to be with them. Learn to imitate those people. Ask the parents, "What did you do to cultivate your children's respect? How did you raise them? What did you teach them?" Ask the children, "What did your parents do that led you to honor them? What do you love about them? Why do you love to spend time with them?" There is much we can learn by inquisitiveness and imitation.

Third, commend your children to the grace of God. Learn to be godly and to imitate worthy models, then commend your children to the grace of God. It is your responsibility to live a life that is worthy of honor, and it is your responsibility to teach your children the importance of honor. But ultimately, honor must be extended by the children, not forced out by the parents. The responsibility falls to your children. They may prove hard-hearted, unwilling to identify the love and grace you've shown them, unwilling to forgive your shortcomings, unwilling to heed God's command. But at least you will have lived a life of honor. You would have fulfilled your God-given duty.

There may be times to appeal to your children when they act dishonorably or, if they are Christians, to even appeal to their church. Church leaders should take seriously every member's responsibility to obey the fifth commandment. Yet in the end, your children will make their own way through life. They will choose to honor God by honoring you, or they will choose to dishonor God by dishonoring you. Even if they choose poorly, you can take comfort in knowing that even if your children forsake you, God will not.

Parents, make it easy for your children to honor you. Make it a delight for them to take pride in you. Live in such a way that your children's glory is truly their parents (Proverbs 17:6).

NOTES

1   Dennis Rainey, *The Forgotten Commandment.*

2   John MacArthur, *Ephesians: MacArthur New Testament Commentary.*

3   John Currid, *A Study Commentary on Deuteronomy.*

4   Dennis Rainey, *The Forgotten Commandment.*

5   https://www.youtube.com/watch?v=26en95whUAk

6   Timothy Keller, *The Timothy Keller Sermon Archive.*

7   Timothy Keller, *The Timothy Keller Sermon Archive.*

8   https://www.cru.org/communities/families/honor-parents-with-tribute.html

9   Bryan Chapell & Kent Hughes, *1 and 2 Timothy and Titus: To Guard the Deposit.*

10   John Stott, *The Message of 1 Timothy & Titus.*

11   https://www.youtube.com/watch?v=p7cOwQQDI7o

12   William Barcley, *A Study Commentary on 1 and 2 Timothy.*

13   T.W. Manson, *The Teaching of Jesus.*

14   Mark Strauss, *Mark.*

15   Douglas Milne, *1 Timothy, 2 Timothy, Titus*; John MacArthur, *1 Timothy: The MacArthur New Testament Commentary.*

16   Douglas Moo, *The Epistle to the Romans.*

17   Eric Lane, *Proverbs: Everyday Wisdom for Everyone.*

18   John Kitchen, *Proverbs: A Mentor Commentary.*

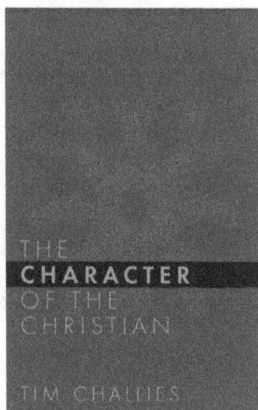

Cruciform Quick booklets by Tim Challies

If you are 16 or 18 or in your 20s, if you are in high school or college or just moving into marriage and career, there are many ways to invest your time, but none is better than the pursuit of godliness. In Paul's letter to young Timothy, you (yes, you!) are called to be an example to your peers and even to older Christians. He calls you to set an example of maturity and godliness in your speech, conduct, love, faith, and purity.

God means for your life to be a canvas, the setting for a beautiful work of art. And he also expects this work of art to be seen, admired, and imitated. Set an example.

The list of qualifications for elders is repeated elsewhere in Scripture as qualities that ought to characterize all believers. Are you growing in godliness? How would you even know?

A good place to begin is understanding and imitating the character qualifications for elders. While elders are meant to exemplify these traits, all Christians are to display them. And with one exception, each is related to character. Study the character of the Christian, and learn to spur one another on to love and good works. Learn to be a model of Christian maturity.

Inductive Bible Studies for Women by Keri Folmar

Endorsed by Kathleen Nielson, Diane Schreiner,
Connie Dever, Kristie Anyabwile, Gloria Furman

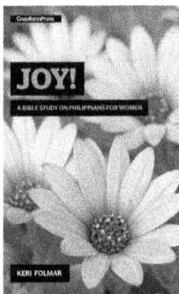

JOY! – A Bible Study
on Philippians
for Women
A 10-week study

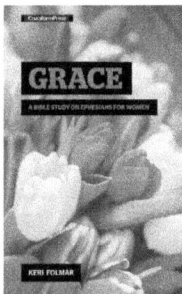

GRACE: A Bible
Study on Ephesians
for Women
A 10-week study

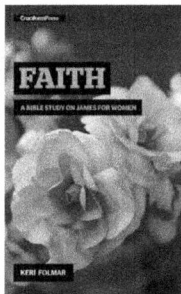

FAITH: A Bible
Study on James
for Women
A 10-week study

A Bible Study for Women on the Gospel of Mark

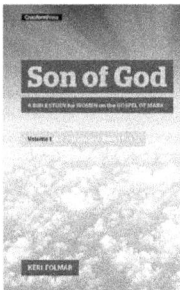

SON OF GOD
Volume 1
An 11-week study

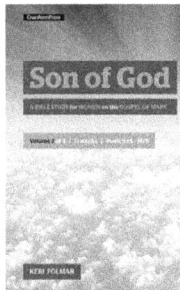

SON OF GOD
Volume 2
An 11-week study

"It is hard to imagine a better inductive Bible Study tool."
–Diane Schreiner

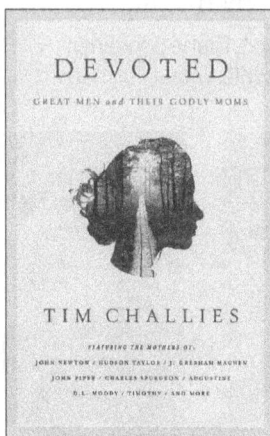

Devoted
Great Men and Their Godly Moms
by Tim Challies

Christian mothers shaped the men who changed the world.

126 pages

Featuring the mothers of John Newton, Hudson Taylor, J. Gresham Machen, John Piper, Charles Spurgeon, Augustine, D.L. Moody, Timothy, and more.

"*Devoted* offers rich encouragement, wisdom, and hope for any mom who longs for her sons and daughters to follow, love, and serve Christ."

Nancy DeMoss Wolgemuth, author, teacher, and host of Revive Our Hearts

"*Devoted* will encourage moms (and dads) in the trenches, but also pour out grace and hope on the parents of prodigals. Reading this book was sheer delight and I highly recommend it."

Kimberly Wagner, author, Fierce Women

"Tim has collected for us the stories of women whose greatness was largely hidden. The devoted lives of thes eleven women will inspire and encourage you. Their stories and examples, so easily overlooked, are now presented in this accessible and helpful book."

Trillia Newbell, author, God's Very Good Idea, and Enjoy

"Challies describes the powerful influence of a godly mother in articulate detail through stories of real women who have gone before us. These women believe the same gospel and cling to the same Christ, and I pray this book encourages many more mothers to follow their lead."

Gloria Furman, author, Missional Motherhood

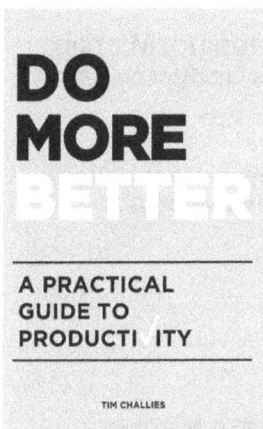

Do More Better

A Practical Guide to Productivity

by Tim Challies

**Don't try to do it all.
Do more good. Better.**

Whether a student or a professional, a work-from-home dad or a stay-at-home mom, this book will help you structure your life to do the most good to the glory of God.

114 pages
bit.ly/domorebetter

Shortly after its release, *Do More Better* had received 173 reviews on Amazon, with an average rating of 4.8 out of 5 stars. The book sold more than 10,000 copies in its first two months. Here are Tim's thoughts about this book:

I am no productivity guru. I am a writer, a church leader, a husband, and a father—a Christian with a lot of responsibilities and with new tasks coming at me all the time. I wrote this short, fast-paced, practical guide to productivity to share what I have learned about getting things done in today's digital world. It will help you learn to structure your life to do the most good to the glory of God.

In Do More Better, you will learn:
- *Common obstacles to productivity*
- *The great purpose behind productivity*
- *3 essential tools for getting things done*
- *The power of daily and weekly routines*
- *And much more, including bonus material on taming your email and embracing the inevitable messiness of productivity.*

It really is possible to live a calm and orderly life, sure of your responsibilities and confident in your progress. You can do more better. And I would love to help you get there. — Tim Challies

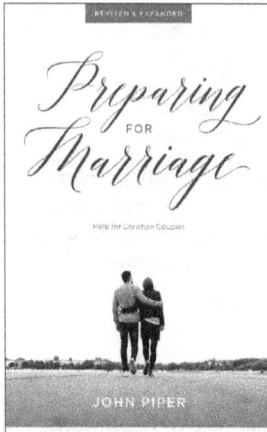

Preparing for Marriage
Help for Christian Couples

by John Piper

As you prepare for marriage, dare to dream with God.

86 pages

Published for Desiring God
by Cruciform Press

http://bit.ly/prep-for-marriage

When preparing for marriage, or even in just beginning to consider it, it can be immensely helpful to have the perspective of someone like John Piper, not only a seasoned husband of nearly 50 years, but also a seasoned pastor, careful thinker, and faithful theologian.

Chapter 1 includes John's counsel about engagement, **chapter 2** about wedding planning (and finances).

Chapter 3 provides invaluable instruction about the beautiful, complementary dynamic the Bible teaches between husband and wife.

Sexual relations in marriage is the topic of **chapter 4.**

In **chapter 5,** John helps us ponder how we can guard our marriages in a day in which they are under assault from every side.

Chapter 6 is based on perhaps John Piper's single most important message on marriage. There he goes more macro than many of us have ever dared to go in thinking about what marriage is, and what God designed it for. This is a glorious, true, life-changing vision.

Appendix 1 contains almost 50 questions to ask each other, in 11 categories, and **Appendix 2** addresses hospitality.